£9.99

AFRICAN
MIGRATIONS

Hakim Adi

Wayland

Titles in the Migrations series

African Migrations   Indian Migrations
Chinese Migrations   Jewish Migrations

The author and publishers would like to thank the following for their
help in writing this book: Aziz Abdulhay, Mohammed Ali, Idris Dirie,
Amina Jama, Amina and Halima Musa, Freweyni Habtemariam and
Oluyemisi Showunmi

First published in 1994 by Wayland (Publishers) Ltd
61 Western Road, Hove, East Sussex, BN3 1JD, England

© Copyright 1994 Wayland (Publishers) Ltd

Editor: Cath Senker
Picture researcher: Shelley Noronha
Series design: Suzie Hooper
Book design: Pardoe Blacker Ltd
Cover design: Simon Borrough
Production controller: Janet Slater

British Library Cataloguing in Publication Data
Adi, Hakim
African Migrations (Migrations series)
I. Title II. Series
304.8096

ISBN 0-7502-1076-1

Printed and bound in Italy by G. Canale & C.S.p.A., Turin

Links with the National Curriculum

HISTORY

KS 2 Core Unit 4: Britain since 1930
Especially chapter 4, which looks at social changes
in Britain.

KS 3 Core Unit 3: Expansion, Trade and
Industry – Britain 1750 to 1900
Especially chapters 2 and 3, which look at the
consequences of empire and slavery.
Core Unit 4: The Twentieth-Century World

KS 3 Supplementary Unit B: a unit involving the study of a
past non-European society, for example, black peoples of
the Americas.

GEOGRAPHY

KS 2 Communications: Journeys
KS 3 Places: Africa
        Population: Migration

The cross-curricular theme of Citizenship, particularly
component 2: A Pluralist Society, and also component 3:
Being a Citizen.

CONTENTS

BRITAIN

London

GERMA

Stu

NORTH

AMERICA

CENTRAL

Caribbean Islands

AMERICA   *CARIBBEAN SEA*

NIGERIA

Lagos

KEY

Main areas of African migration

Countries mentioned in the modern case studies:

Migration from

Migration to

SOUTH

AMERICA

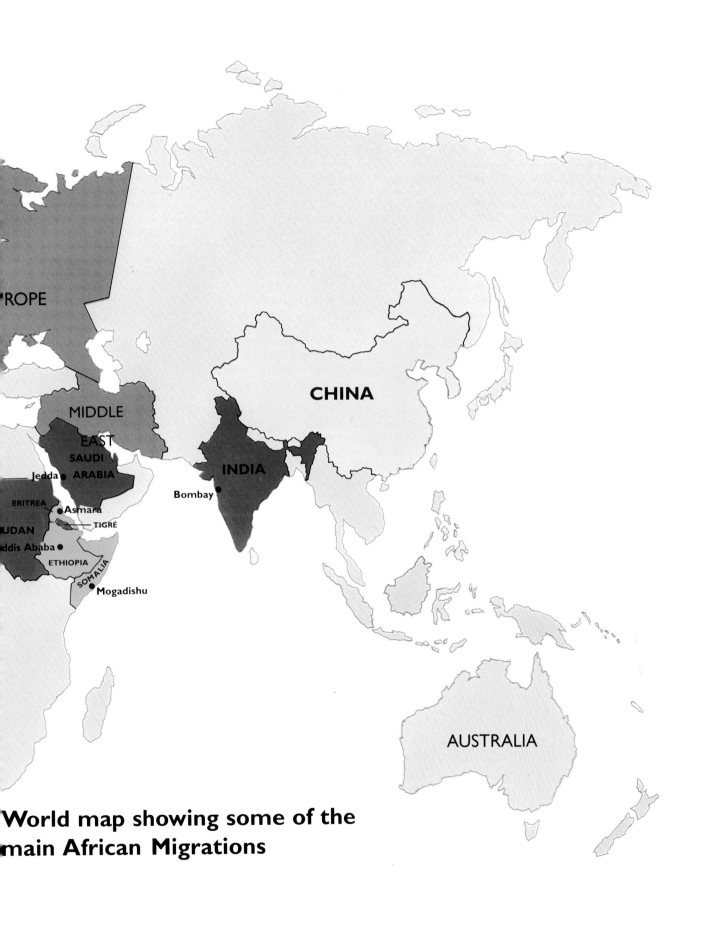

ROPE

MIDDLE

EAST

SAUDI

Jedda • ARABIA

ERITREA

• Asmara

TIGRÉ

UDAN

ddis Ababa •

ETHIOPIA

SOMALIA

• Mogadishu

CHINA

INDIA

Bombay •

AUSTRALIA

World map showing some of the
main African Migrations

1 Introduction

Today Africans can be found in every continent of the world. Large African communities live in Britain, France, Germany, Italy and in many other countries of Western Europe. There are Africans in China, India and Australia and throughout the Middle East. Millions of Africans live in North, Central and South America, and in the Caribbean.

Why have so many Africans left Africa? How did over 20 million African-Americans come to live in the USA? How are many people from the Caribbean linked to Africa? What is the connection between them and recently-arrived immigrants from Somalia or Nigeria? These pages will help you to answer these questions for yourself. But first we need to know something about Africa, its peoples and its history.

A map of Africa showing the geographical features.

Sand dunes in Salah, Algeria.

Dar es Salaam harbour in Tanzania, East Africa.

Sudd

River Nile

rasslands

Ethiopian Highlands

Congo

ests

Lake Victoria

Rift valley

Lake Tanganyika

Lake Nyasa

Central Plateau

River Zambezi

Savanna Grasslands

AHARI

SERT

River Orange

thern plateau

The continent of Africa is the second largest in the world and in 1994 had a population of over 500 million people. It is 3.5 times the size of the USA and larger than China and India put together. Over 1,500 different languages are spoken there. Today Africa is divided into fifty-four different countries, so that even in one country there are often many different peoples (often wrongly called tribes), each speaking their own language.

Because Africa is so large it has a great variety of climates and differing landscapes. It contains mountains and highlands, great river valleys, deserts and beaches alongside great oceans, fertile farmland and small villages. And of course great crowded cities, full of skyscrapers, traffic jams and noise.

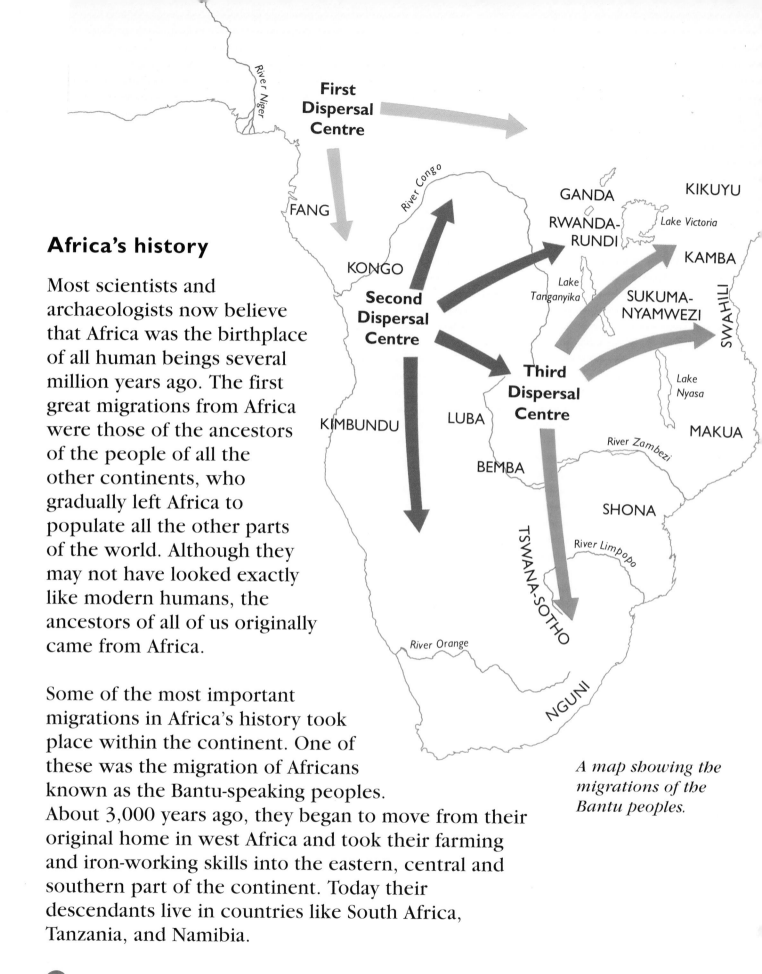

Africa's history

Most scientists and archaeologists now believe that Africa was the birthplace of all human beings several million years ago. The first great migrations from Africa were those of the ancestors of the people of all the other continents, who gradually left Africa to populate all the other parts of the world. Although they may not have looked exactly like modern humans, the ancestors of all of us originally came from Africa.

Some of the most important migrations in Africa's history took place within the continent. One of these was the migration of Africans known as the Bantu-speaking peoples. About 3,000 years ago, they began to move from their original home in west Africa and took their farming and iron-working skills into the eastern, central and southern part of the continent. Today their descendants live in countries like South Africa, Tanzania, and Namibia.

First Dispersal Centre

Second Dispersal Centre

Third Dispersal Centre

FANG

KONGO

KIMBUNDU

LUBA

BEMBA

TSWANA-SOTHO

NGUNI

GANDA

RWANDA-RUNDI

KIKUYU

KAMBA

SUKUMA-NYAMWEZI

SWAHILI

MAKUA

SHONA

River Niger

River Congo

Lake Victoria

Lake Tanganyika

Lake Nyasa

River Zambezi

River Limpopo

River Orange

A map showing the migrations of the Bantu peoples.

The migrations that have taken place within Africa, such as that of the Bantu-speaking peoples, have often meant great hardships and many years and kilometres of travel for the people involved. People have found it necessary to move for different reasons; perhaps to find more fertile land for farming, or better grazing for their cattle or camels. Or like many modern migrants, they might have moved to work or to trade, or because of wars or other dangers that made it unsafe to remain where they were.

Today many people think of Africa only as a continent of war, poverty and famine. But this is not the whole story. For thousands of years, before most of Africa was conquered and ruled by European countries, it had powerful kingdoms and great civilizations; for example that of ancient Egypt, 5,000 years ago.

Many historians now think that the ancient Greeks gained much of their knowledge from Egypt. Important ideas from Egypt may also have spread to other parts of Africa and even to parts of Spain, where there were African rulers and peoples from 711 to 1492.

Two of Egypt's great monuments – a pyramid and the Sphinx. The Sphinx is thought to be a statue of Pharaoh Kephren, who lived over 4,500 years ago.

A European map (1375) of West Africa, showing the Emperor of Mali (seated), one of the world's richest and most powerful rulers.

Six hundred years ago the empire of Mali, in West Africa, was said to be one of the biggest, richest and best-governed countries in the world. Arabs and Europeans who travelled to Africa hundreds of years ago usually reported how Africa had well-designed and organized cities, like Timbuktu or Kilwa, which traded with countries as far away as China.

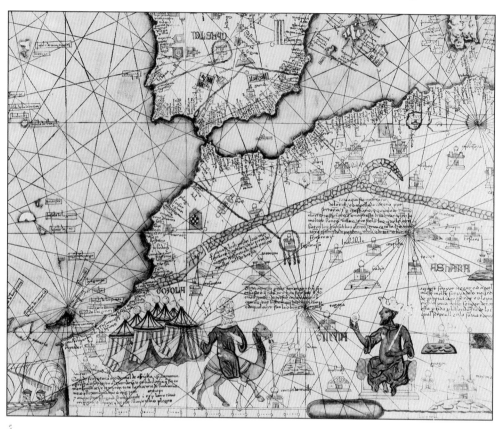

(Right) Mosque in Jenne, once one of the most important towns in the empire of Mali.

The trade links that Africans had with Arabs and Europeans hundreds of years ago sometimes included the sale of human beings. Slavery and the slave trade were once common in many parts of the world, including Europe. African slaves were regularly taken to the Middle East, Europe and India. Then, about five hundred years ago, the first African slaves were taken by Europeans to those areas they had conquered in North, Central and South America and in the Caribbean. This transatlantic slave trade led to terrible wars and great suffering in Africa. Many people were killed, and towns and villages were destroyed. Millions of people, from different parts of the continent, were violently captured and shipped in terrible conditions, to places thousands of kilometres away. Most of them never returned home.

PART 1 Africans in the Americas

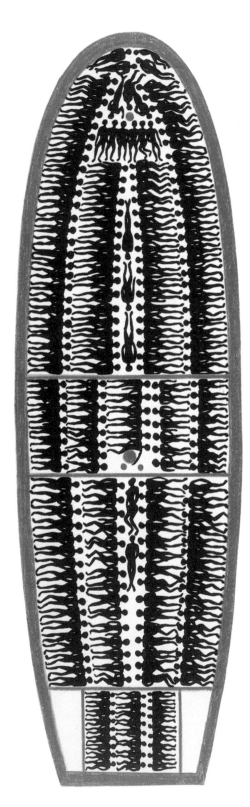

Plan of one deck of a slave ship taking slaves to America.

2 Forced migration to North America 1500 – 1900

The Atlantic Slave Trade

For 400 years after Christopher Columbus first landed in the American continent in 1492, millions of Africans were taken there to work as slaves growing sugar, cotton and tobacco. Slaves also worked as miners, soldiers, shipbuilders, and in many other jobs.

Some African rulers such as Queen Nzingha, who ruled Ndongo in the seventeenth century (a kingdom in what is today Angola), tried to stop the trade in slaves. Others tried not to take part in it. But there was a great demand for slaves in those parts of the American continent which had been conquered by countries such as Spain, Portugal, Britain and France. There were always some African rulers and traders who were prepared to capture and sell slaves to make themselves rich.

The Atlantic Slave Trade is sometimes called the 'Triangular Trade'. The three points of the triangle were Europe, Africa and America. The slave traders were able to make a profit at each of these three points. The wealth from the slave trade was used to finance the industrial revolution in Europe.

The unpaid work of Africans helped to make the European countries that carried out the slave trade rich and powerful. It also benefited all those areas conquered by Europeans in the American continent. The USA owes much of its present wealth to the work of African slaves and their descendants. Africa on the other hand, gained nothing of any value, and lost millions of its population, especially from parts of West Africa. Many countries of Africa were weakened by the slave trade and became unable to develop their economies. European countries gradually interfered more and more in African affairs. In the nineteenth century they began the conquest of most of Africa, which was divided up and ruled by European countries.

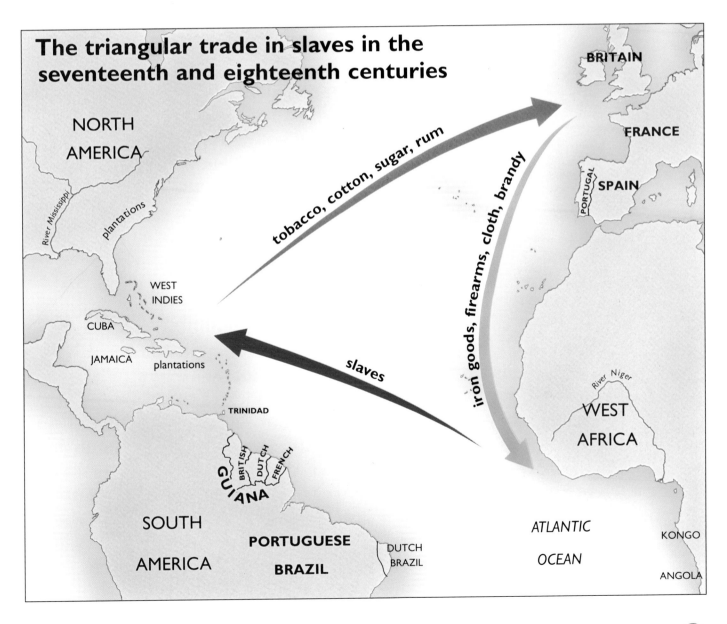

The triangular trade in slaves in the seventeenth and eighteenth centuries

NORTH AMERICA

River Mississippi

plantations

WEST INDIES

CUBA

JAMAICA   plantations

TRINIDAD

BRITISH   DUTCH   FRENCH
GUIANA

SOUTH AMERICA

PORTUGUESE BRAZIL

DUTCH BRAZIL

tobacco, cotton, sugar, rum

iron goods, firearms, cloth, brandy

slaves

BRITAIN

FRANCE

PORTUGAL   SPAIN

River Niger

WEST AFRICA

ATLANTIC OCEAN

KONGO

ANGOLA

OLAUDAH EQUIANO

In 1756 Olaudah Equiano and his sister were kidnapped from their village in Nigeria, West Africa. Olaudah was just eleven years old, but he was separated from his sister and taken as a slave by an African blacksmith. Equiano had several other African owners before he was taken to the coast and put on board a slave ship which took him to Barbados in the Caribbean. Then he was taken to Virginia in North America, where he was sold to work on a tobacco plantation.

After many difficulties, Olaudah was able to buy his own freedom. He later moved to Britain and became one of the most famous opponents of the slave trade there. He wrote a book about his life which describes all the evils of the slave trade and slavery.

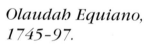

Olaudah Equiano, 1745-97.

Some historians have found evidence which suggests that Africans may have travelled to the American continent before Europeans even knew that it existed, possibly even in the time of the ancient Egyptians. Statues, pyramids and pottery found in Mexico seem to be similar to those found in Africa. Columbus had visited West Africa before his journey to America and had taken African sailors with him. When he reached America the Native Americans said that they had already seen African people. In West Africa there are reports from over 600 years ago which tell of voyages across the Atlantic in the direction of America. The tides and winds would have made such journeys possible. [1]

Historians have estimated that by the time the slave trade ended in the 1880s, at least 30 million Africans may have been taken from the continent.[2] Some 15 million Africans arrived alive in North, Central and South America, and in the islands of the Caribbean. European demand for slaves led to one of the greatest forced migrations ever known.

Slave resistance and revolts

Africans never stopped trying to free themselves from slavery. They fought to defend themselves against kidnapping, and tried to escape from the slave ships.

In 1839 Africans travelling to Cuba on board the Spanish slave ship *L'Amistad* killed the captain and some of the crew and tried to sail back to Sierra Leone. The Africans were led by a man called Joseph Cinque, who was said to be an African prince. They were tricked and recaptured along the coast of the USA, but finally freed by the US Supreme Court. Joseph Cinque told the other Africans:

'I am resolved that it is better to die than be a white man's slave, and I will not complain if by dying I save you.'

Joseph Cinque, leader of the L'Amistad *rebellion.*

Slaves had no rights – they could be whipped or even killed by their owners. Children were often taken from their mothers and sold to other owners. Once they were in the USA, slaves such as Nat Turner and Denmark Vesey organized rebellions and tried to escape. In 1831 Nat Turner led a rebellion across the state of Virginia. Slave owners were killed and their slaves freed. Finally Nat Turner was captured and killed. After the rebellion slave owners did everything they could to stop slaves from meeting together. Slaves were even forbidden to pray together.

A painting showing the capture of Nat Turner.

The Underground Railroad

Some slaves were freed when their owners died, or like Equiano they were able to buy their freedom. With the help of some white Americans who disagreed with slavery they formed an organization called the Underground Railroad to help other slaves escape. The Railroad was made up of people who would help by hiding slaves in their homes, or show them how to travel north to Canada, where they would be free.

Sojourner Truth (1797–1883), a leader of the anti-slavery movement.

HARRIET TUBMAN

Harriet Tubman was born into slavery in 1823 in Maryland. When she was twenty-five years old she escaped from the plantation where she worked and was helped by the Underground Railway to reach Canada. She returned to Maryland in 1850 to rescue her parents. She then made eighteen more trips to help to rescue 300 other slaves.

Harriet Tubman (with pan) and some of the slaves she helped to escape.

Plantation owners offered a $50,000 reward for her capture, but she was never caught.

During the American Civil War Harriet became a scout and nurse for the Union army, which fought to end slavery in the USA. She once said: 'I had reasoned this out in my mind; there was one of two things I had a right to, liberty or death; if I could not have one, I would have the other.'

African-American culture

The slave owners tried to mix Africans from different nations together so that it would be hard for them to unite and rebel. Slaves were forced to change their African names and were given European names by their owners. However, Africans resisted and coped with slavery not only by rebelling and escaping but also by developing their own music, religious beliefs and languages. These helped them to deal with everyday life. From the many African cultures the slaves and free African-Americans created new African-American ways of speaking, of telling stories, and cooking food. Some African traditions such as hair plaiting never died out.

An eighteenth-century painting showing slaves in the USA. One is playing the banjo, originally an African instrument.

The music and songs of African slaves were a very important way of keeping alive hope for future freedom. They also often included memories of Africa. This song was still being sung by slaves in the 1840s:

See these poor souls from Africa
Transported to America
We are stolen, and sold to Georgia
Will you go along with me?
Come sound the jubilee!

See wives and husbands sold apart,
Their children's screams will break my heart
There's a better day a coming
Will you go along with me?
There's a better day a coming,
Go sound the jubilee! [3]

Some slaves became Christians, but they often mixed Christianity with religious ideas brought from Africa. Slaves often used stories from the Bible in their songs. These songs are called spirituals and are much more than just religious songs. Stories from the Bible were used to cover up the real meaning of the songs, which were often about hopes of freedom and the end of slavery.

A new language

Historians have discovered over 4,000 African words which are still being used by African-American people called the Gullah, who live in parts of South Carolina, Florida and Georgia, USA. Most slaves were forced to forget their African languages, so they had to speak English. But they spoke English in their own way and still used some African words. African-American words such as 'guy', meaning a man, 'tote', meaning carry, 'cooter', meaning tortoise and 'OK', meaning alright, are still with us today.

African-American food

Africans brought with them to the USA food such as black-eyed beans, water-melons, yams, okra, sesame and red peppers. In some parts of the USA sesame is still called by the African name of *benne*. The gumbo, a well-known soup or stew from the southern part of the USA, takes its name from *ngombo*, an Angolan word for okra.

Here you can see African foods such as water-melons, yams and peppers.

Benjamin Banneker 1731–1806.

Inventors

Both during and after slavery, which was finally abolished in the USA in 1863, African-Americans have made important contributions to life in the USA. Benjamin Banneker, born in 1731, was a free African-American inventor and scientist. He helped to choose the site for the White House and plan the layout of Washington D.C., the capital of the USA.

Elijah McCoy, the son of runaway slaves, was another famous inventor. He invented over seventy-five different parts for machines and trains. He gave his name to the expression 'the real McCoy'. Lewis Latimer, who worked with Alexander Graham Bell and Thomas Edison, helped to invent the electric light bulb.

Racism and discrimination in the twentieth century

Many years after slavery was abolished, African-Americans were still discriminated against in many areas of life. Until the 1960s, in most southern states African-Americans were forced to use separate, inferior facilities. They used separate public water-fountains, restaurants, schools, and even seats on buses. This was called segregation.

A segregated drinking fountain.

African-Americans were prevented from voting and were attacked and killed by racist organizations such as the Ku-Klux-Klan. The Ku-Klux-Klan and some other white Americans have never accepted that African-Americans should have the same rights as whites. They believe that black people are inferior to white people.

The Civil Rights movement

During the 1950s and 1960s millions of African-Americans protested about the way they were treated in the USA. They refused to accept separate and inferior facilities, and campaigned for equal rights. This was known as the Civil Rights movement. Eventually some laws were changed so that segregation and discrimination in jobs and housing were made illegal.

Martin Luther King (second from left), leading a demonstration in the 1960s.

Today some African-Americans are scientists or doctors, and a few are important politicians, such as Jesse Jackson, or well-known writers, such as Toni Morrison. African-Americans make up over 13 per cent of the US population – over 25 million people – but many feel that they are still discriminated against. A large number live in very poor housing and work in the lowest-paid jobs.

Nobel Prize winner Toni Morrison, signing one of her books, 1993.

African-Americans and their links with Africa

Many African-Americans have retained their links with Africa. As early as 1806, Paul Cuffe, a free African-American from Massachusetts who was a wealthy shipowner, travelled to West Africa to trade and to take African-Americans who wished to resettle in Sierra Leone. Some 20,000 African-Americans settled in Liberia, West Africa in the nineteenth century.

In 1859 Martin Delany, a doctor and campaigner against slavery, visited Liberia and what is today Nigeria. He signed an agreement with the Alake (King) of Abeokuta, which allowed African-Americans to return and settle in this part of Nigeria.

Marcus Garvey was born in Jamaica in 1887. He was a descendant of the Maroons (see page 26). He later travelled throughout the Caribbean and Central America, and in 1912 visited London. Everywhere he went he saw that black people were mistreated and lived in the poorest conditions. In 1914 Garvey returned to Jamaica and started the Universal Negro Improvement Association (UNIA). In 1916 he moved to New York, started a UNIA branch there, and published a newspaper called *Negro World*.

During the twentieth century many more African-Americans have become interested in their links with Africa. Because of slavery and racism many African-Americans had forgotten about Africa, or did not want to admit that their ancestors were Africans. They had not been told the truth about the African continent. All over the world people were taught that Africa was a continent of jungles and savages. They were even told that great civilizations, such as that of ancient Egypt, were not African. Africans, it was said, were not capable of creating anything of value.

This boy of African origin is proud to wear African clothes.

MARCUS GARVEY

Marcus Garvey (right) and two members of UNIA, in 1924.

Throughout the 1920s Marcus Garvey encouraged Jamaicans, African-Americans and people throughout the African diaspora to identify with Africa and return there if possible.
His ideas and his slogan 'Africa for the Africans at home and abroad', was very popular in Africa too. Many people hoped that Garvey and the UNIA would help to free them and their countries from European rule. After his death Marcus Garvey was honoured as one of Jamaica's National Heroes.

Malcolm X

In the 1960s Malcolm X, the famous African-American political leader, also spoke of the importance of Africa. He told African-Americans to be proud of their African past and to learn more about Africa's history. Malcolm X said they should support the people of Africa who were fighting for independence from European rule. He told African-Americans who wanted nothing to do with Africa: 'You can't hate Africa and not hate yourself.'

Malcolm X (1925–65) speaking during the 1960s.

A photo of the actor playing Kunta Kinte, one of the heroes of the film Roots.

Roots

In 1976, the African-American writer Alex Haley had a book published called *Roots: The Saga of an American Family*. This book became famous and was later made into a television series. It traces the story of his own family who were descendants of an African slave taken to America in 1767. Alex Haley told the story of 200 years of African-American life in the United States. He believed that he had been able to trace his own family back to a village in the West African country of Gambia. Haley visited the village and met people whom he believed were his distant cousins.

3 The Caribbean, Central and South America from 1500

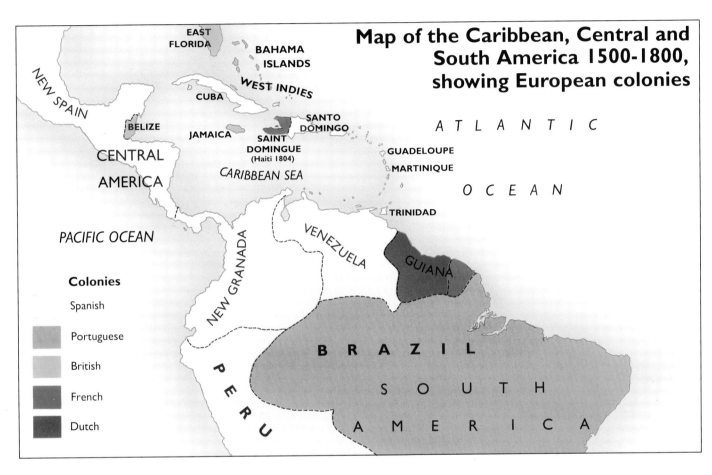

Map of the Caribbean, Central and South America 1500-1800, showing European colonies

EAST FLORIDA

NEW SPAIN

BAHAMA ISLANDS

WEST INDIES

CUBA

BELIZE

JAMAICA

SANTO DOMINGO

SAINT DOMINGUE (Haiti 1804)

CENTRAL AMERICA

CARIBBEAN SEA

GUADELOUPE

MARTINIQUE

A T L A N T I C

O C E A N

TRINIDAD

PACIFIC OCEAN

VENEZUELA

NEW GRANADA

GUIANA

PERU

B R A Z I L

S O U T H

A M E R I C A

Colonies

Spanish

Portuguese

British

French

Dutch

As well as being taken to North America, large numbers of African slaves were taken to the islands in the Caribbean and to Central and South America from the end of the fifteenth century. In most Caribbean countries today the descendants of Africans make up the majority of the population.

In the Caribbean and Central and South America, Europeans and native Americans were the first people to be used as slaves. But as the demand for labour grew, more African slaves were imported. Africans had many skills as miners, cattle herders and farmers. They were used to grow tobacco, sugar, cotton and other valuable crops.

In the Caribbean islands, African slaves and their descendants soon outnumbered the slave owners and the few other Europeans who had conquered and ruled these countries. In parts of South America, such as Brazil, there were also large number of African slaves. In these areas there was always the possibility of slave rebellion.

SLAVE REBELLIONS AND REVOLTS

The Republic of Palmares

In Brazil from the seventeenth century onwards, African runaway slaves created *quilombos* (originally an African word meaning a war camp, it came to mean a camp of runaway slaves). The most famous was the Republic of Palmares, which was founded in 1605 and had a population of 10,000 people. The Portuguese and Dutch, who were both fighting to rule Brazil, tried to conquer it more than twenty times during the seventeenth century. Palmares was run by an elected African chief called the *Ganga Zumba* (Great Lord) and had its own laws. In 1678 the *Ganga Zumba* agreed to a peace treaty with the Portuguese. But war started again in 1680 and Palmares was captured by the Portuguese in 1694.

The Maroons and the British Army during peace talks in 1739.

Jamaican Maroons

In Jamaica there were more slave rebellions than in any other Caribbean island, especially after Britain conquered the island from Spain in 1655, and began to bring in many more slaves. The runaway slaves were called Maroons by the British (from the Spanish *cimarrón* meaning 'untamed').

Toussaint L'Ouverture (1743–1803), known by the French as the 'Black Napoleon'.

The Maroons also set up their own societies and had their own laws. Each Maroon village was led by an *Osofu*, or village council. Women as well as men could be rulers. One of the most famous women leaders was Nanny. The Maroons fought many wars against the British.

Finally in 1739, they signed a peace treaty in which the British recognized their leaders and allowed them to live freely and to own land. But the Maroons also agreed to return future runaways to their owners. The Maroons retained African names and kept alive many African traditions, especially their belief in *obeah*, or magic.

Toussaint L'Ouverture and independent Haiti

There was a successful rebellion in the French colony in the Caribbean called Saint Domingue, said then to be the most valuable colony in the world because of the sugar that was grown there. Led by the resistance fighter Toussaint L'Ouverture (which in French means 'the opening'), the African slaves freed the entire island from British, Spanish and French rule. In 1804 they established an independent Haiti, the first modern republic to be governed by Africans.

Haiti came to be seen as the symbol of African achievement by Africans all over the world.

African culture

The large numbers of Africans in the Caribbean and in some areas of Central and South America led to the growth of new but often distinctly African cultures. These cultures include the traditions of the native American peoples, as well as those of other people who have migrated to this area from Europe, India and China.

But African traditions remain very strong. In new religions such as the Candomble of Brazil, and Shango of Trinidad, the Yoruba language from Nigeria is still used. The Kumina religion of Jamaica is thought to have come originally from Zaire, in central Africa. In some countries, such as Surinam, people still use many African words in their language.

An English painting from 1810 showing African music and dance in the Caribbean island of Dominica.

The languages spoken by Africans in the Caribbean are usually based on European languages such as English and French. But the African slaves, who originally spoke many different languages, developed new ones so they could speak together. Today these languages are sometimes called Creole languages, or in some countries 'patois'. They may still contain some

African words, or have been influenced by African grammar. Language was just one way in which Africans kept alive their own culture.

The songs of slaves show clearly how they still thought of their African homeland. This song, which uses patois, was heard in Jamaica around 1790. Ebo, Guinea and Congo were all parts of the West African coast, the former homes of the slaves. The song explains that the slaves are unable to return to their homes since they have been kidnapped.

If me want for go in a Ebo,
Me can't go there!
Since dem tief [kidnapped] me
from a Guinea,
Me can't go there!

If me want for go in a Congo
Me can't go there!
Since dem tief me from my tatta
[grandmother/close relative]
Me can't go there! [4]

Caribbean music, such as reggae and calypso, shows many different influences. The word 'calypso' is thought to come from the West African word *kaiso*, which was shouted to encourage musicians. The originally Christian festival of carnival was taken over by the freed slaves in Trinidad in the nineteenth century. They changed it into a popular festival of song and dance.

Modern carnival in Trinidad.

Back to Africa

In the nineteenth century some free Africans in South America and the Caribbean made attempts to return home. Afro-Brazilians and Afro-Cubans returned to West Africa. Barbadians and Jamaicans also returned to West Africa, taking their skills with them. Some returned as soldiers or missionaries, others as traders and builders.

A Rastafarian family in Jamaica.

More recently, the Jamaican-based Rastafarian movement has become popular among many people of African origin in the Caribbean and throughout the world.

The movement was based on some of the ideas of Marcus Garvey. The Rastafarians also believe in returning to Africa, especially to Ethiopia, which they think was the ancient home of all African people. The Rastafarians wear the colours of the Ethiopian flag, red, gold and green.

In the twentieth century many people from the Caribbean have become migrants. Caribbean countries have remained poor, so some people have left and gone to live and work in countries such as Britain, France and the USA.

PART 2

Modern migrations

In the twentieth century many Africans have become migrants for economic and political reasons. Africans are no longer forced to migrate as they were during the time of the slave trade. However, African countries did not develop during the time they were ruled by European countries. Even during the last thirty years when most have become independent, they have remained poor with many social and political problems.

A ship carrying 2,000 Somali refugees arriving in Yemen in 1992.

Some Africans have travelled abroad as students and then decided to stay in order to find work. Other African migrants were seamen or workers who decided to migrate because their own countries were poor and they wanted to find a better life.

After 1945 many Africans were encouraged to travel to countries in Europe, such as France, Italy and Britain, where there was a shortage of workers. More recently, many migrants have left countries such as Somalia and Eritrea as refugees from wars.

The following four chapters tell the stories of some of these modern African migrants.

4 Moving from Nigeria to Britain 1960 – 80

From the 1950s and 1960s many Nigerians migrated to Britain. Throughout the twentieth century until 1960 Nigeria had been ruled by Britain. Many Nigerians thought that Britain was the best place to go to be educated or to find a job and a better life. Yemisi came to Britain from Nigeria in 1967, when she was ten years old. She came to join her mother and father who had left Nigeria five years before. Yemisi had been brought up by her grandmother in Lagos, the capital of Nigeria.

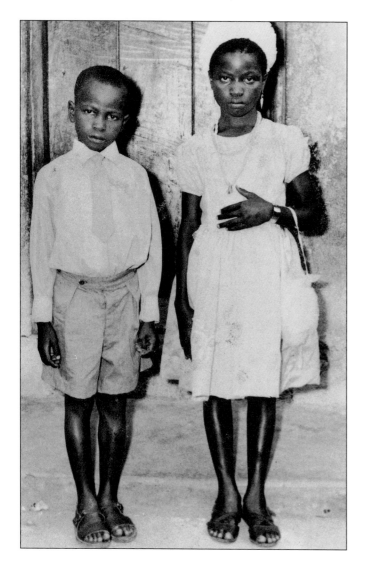

Yemisi did not want to leave her grandmother. She had almost forgotten about her mother and father who were living in London. The only good thing about leaving was that she had a new dress, hat and handbag for the journey.

Yemisi and her eight-year-old brother flew to London alone. Yemisi's father met them at the airport, but they did not recognize him at first. London seemed very grey and quiet, unlike Lagos, which was noisy and colouful. Yemisi started to miss her grandmother and Nigeria straight away.

Yemisi and her brother just before they left Nigeria.

Yemisi's father had been a student, but when she arrived he was working as an electrician. Yemisi's mother, who had also wanted to study, was a factory worker.

Yemisi had been poor in Lagos. She had lived in one room with her family, including her grandmother, great-grandmother and aunt. They had all slept on the floor. When Yemisi came to London her parents were still living in one small room. She and her brother joined them. They all slept in one bed, and had to share the kitchen and bathroom

Yemisi (back left) aged nine, with her aunt and other children, in Nigeria.

with all the other people who lived in the house. There was no central heating and in the winter Yemisi and her family keep warm around a small paraffin heater.

One week after she arrived in London Yemisi and her brother started school. Even though Yemisi had only just arrived in Britain, her mother gave her a door key so that she could come home from school on her own.

Migrants sometimes find it hard to settle in at school.

Yemisi found life at school difficult for some time. She had had to speak English at school in Nigeria so she could understand her lessons. But the other children made fun of her accent. Some tried to undo her hair which was bound with thread in a traditional way. Sometimes she had to fight other children to make them stop bullying her.

A Nigerian family in Britain, wearing traditional Nigerian clothes.

Yemisi found life in Britain very different from her old life in Nigeria. When she had lived with her grandmother, she had to get up at five o'clock to go and fetch water from the well. She helped her grandmother prepare food to sell at the market. Then Yemisi walked all the way to school barefoot in the hot sun.

In Nigeria, Yemisi had learnt English at school, but at home she spoke Yoruba. In London she was encouraged by her parents to speak English most of the time, even at home. After a few years Yemisi's younger brother forgot how to speak Yoruba. Yemisi did her best to remember her language even when she did not hear it regularly.

In the 1960s it was not easy to buy Nigerian food in London. Even rice was not as common as it is today. Vegetables such as yam and okra were seldom seen. When they could, Yemisi and her family would eat *eba*, *apon*, and *ewedu*.

Eba is made from ground cassava and mixed with hot water to make a kind of starchy dough. This is eaten with a meat or fish stew. Nigerians in London sometimes used semolina or ground rice instead, as these were easier to buy in Britain.

Yemisi thought that many things she saw in London were strange. She was surprised to see so many old people doing their own shopping. In Nigeria their shopping would be done by younger family members.

Yemisi (left) and her daughter (right) on a visit to Nigeria in 1987.

Yemisi spent the next sixteen years in London. When she first returned to Nigeria to visit her grandmother in 1983, she had two children of her own. Although she has spent so many years in Britain, Yemisi says that she still feels like an immigrant. She always feels much more at home in Nigeria. When her children have grown up she hopes to return to live in the land of her birth.

5 Ethiopian refugees go to Saudi Arabia 1980s

Many people from the Horn of Africa migrate to the countries of the Middle East. Indeed there have been strong trading links between these two areas for thousands of years. Between 523–525 parts of Arabia were ruled by Ethiopian kings. After the birth of the religion of Islam in the seventh century, many Africans travelled to Arabia on pilgrimage, as Muslims do today.

The city of Asmara, the capital of Eritrea.

Aziz was born in Asmara, the capital of Eritrea, but his parents are from Tigré in northern Ethiopia. Because there was little work in Ethiopia, they migrated to Eritrea in the 1960s before Aziz was born. But life in Eritrea was also very hard and there was little work. At that time the Eritreans were fighting for their independence from Ethiopia.

Aziz's father left home to find work and when he was seven his mother migrated to Saudi Arabia, where she hoped to find work as a housemaid. Aziz stayed with his grandparents until he was eleven years old, then he was sent to stay with his older brother who was living in Sudan.

After nearly two years in Sudan, Aziz's mother was able to send the visa and the money he needed to travel to join her in Saudi Arabia. A friend of his mother's took him to the airport for his flight to Jedda, the largest city in Saudi Arabia.

Aziz was met at Jedda by his mother. He soon saw how modern the city was. Everybody seemed to be driving cars and there were new buildings everywhere.

The modern city of Jedda.

Children from many countries go to this school in Saudi Arabia.

Saudi Arabia is a Muslim country. Aziz was a Muslim and he had spent two years in Sudan, another Muslim country, so the Islamic customs did not surprise him. But the rules were stricter in Saudi Arabia. For example, men and women there are not supposed to mix together in public. Boys and girls learn in separate schools. Soon Aziz started at his new all-boys school.

Aziz had been learning Arabic in Sudan, but he found that the Arabic spoken in Saudi Arabia was so different that it was almost like learning another new language. He also found it difficult to make friends with the local children.

There were almost 80,000 Eritreans and Tigréans (from northern Ethiopia) in Saudi Arabia. About half of these lived in Jedda. They were usually well treated there, but they only got low-paid and unskilled jobs.

A woman preparing injera *in Tigré.*

Tigréan culture

Aziz and his younger brother soon after they arrived in Jedda.

Aziz and his family continued to speak their own language, Tigrinya, in Saudi Arabia. They also often ate their own Tigréan food such as *injera* (a flat bread like a pancake) with *zegni*, a hot, spicy sauce.

In Saudi Arabia, weddings were the most important occasions for Eritreans and Tigréans. Even though they were living in a Muslim country, men and women were able to mix freely together to enjoy traditional dancing and music played on the *kerar*, a small five-stringed harp, and *kebero*, a small drum which looks like a tambourine.

Even though there were other Ethiopians in Jedda, most were much older than Aziz and he often felt lonely. It was hard to get used to living with his mother and brothers again after so many years spent apart. Although he stayed in Saudi Arabia for six years he was never really happy there.

6 Eritrean refugees move to Germany 1990s

The war between Ethiopia and Eritrea meant that many people became refugees and had to leave the country to avoid the fighting. Freweyni was born in 1967 in a village close to Asmara, the capital of Eritrea. She moved as a baby to Addis Ababa, the capital of Ethiopia, where she lived until 1975. Then she went back to Eritrea, but because of the fighting the family spent the next four years moving from town to town.

A camp for Eritrean and Ethiopian refugees in Kassala, Sudan.

In 1979 Freweyni, her mother, sister and three brothers left Eritrea and went to Kassala, a town in Sudan close to the border of Eritrea.

It took them three weeks by camel. Planes bombed the roads throughout their journey, so it was safer to travel at night.

Freweyni and her family did not know anybody in Kassala, but an Eritrean woman saw them and realized they were refugees. She brought them home, and a few days later the woman took them to a friend of Freweyni's father. He gave them a room in his house to stay in.

Eritreans at the refugee centre in Karlsruhe, Germany in 1987.

After three months Freweyni and her family were able to travel to Germany. It was very difficult for Eritreans to get a passport and visa.

It was the first time that Freweyni had ever been on a plane so she was very excited by the journey. But when she and her family arrived at Stuttgart airport everything was new and frightening. Because Freweyni's youngest brother and sister were ill, her mother went with them to the hospital. Freweyni and her two other brothers had to go on their own to the Red Cross home for refugees.

After three weeks Freweyni's family were moved to a refugee camp at Karlsruhe. At that time the German Government helped people who had to leave their own countries, so at the camp there were other refugees from all over the world. Freweyni hated the place. She and her family could not eat the food they were given and were always hungry or ill. They found it difficult to understand what was said to them. Fortunately, some students from the local university used to come to the camp to try and teach them German. Sometimes they would take Freweyni for walks and show her around the town.

Just as they were getting used to the camp and making some friends they were moved to another town called Bad Worzach, about three hours drive from Stuttgart. But when they arrived there was nowhere for them to go. They had to live in an old people's home for the next three months. They were the only Eritreans in the town and felt very lonely. Life was very difficult in the home.

There are people from many countries living in Germany.

The food was prepared for old people, and not suitable for children. Freweyni's brothers and sister had nowhere to play.

Freweyni and her brothers were sent to local schools. The German children were friendly but were always asking them lots of questions: Why were they in Germany? What was Africa like? They felt different from everybody else.

Freweyni's father soon joined them in Germany, and later the family moved into a house in the town centre. They still found it very difficult to get used to Germany. Freweyni made some German friends, but she missed seeing other Eritreans. Freweyni and her family were eventually able to contact other Eritreans in Germany. Every few weeks they would meet to talk about their lives as refugees and about Eritrea. Freweyni often wrote to her aunts and uncles in Eritrea, but she was not able to visit until Eritrea finally won independence from Ethiopia in 1991.

Eritrean refugee at a carpentry class, Berlin.

Freweyni and her family still live in Germany. In 1994 there were more than 18,000 Eritreans living there. But life has become much more difficult for refugees and other migrants.

Some Germans are blaming migrants for all the problems in the country and saying there are too many Africans. Some refugees have been attacked and even killed.

Freweyni and her family have always done everything they could to make friends with Germans. Now they feel that they are unwelcome in Germany and hope that soon they can return to Eritrea.

7 Somalis migrate to India 1990s

For many hundreds of years people from Somalia, Ethiopia and other parts of the Horn of Africa have been travelling to India. Many Africans in India were soldiers or slaves but some were famous kings and generals. Five hundred years ago there were African kings in Bengal.

Africans known as *Siddis* settled on Janjira Island near Bombay, and for hundreds of years chose their own kings. The most famous African in India's history was the Ethiopian Malik Ambar, a former slave who in 1602 became ruler of the Indian kingdom of Ahmadnagar.

Today Africans still migrate to India. Mohammed Ali was born in Erigavo, a town in northern Somalia. He went to school in Mogadishu, the capital of Somalia, until he was eighteen. Because of the civil war in his country Mohammed was unable to return to his home town. If he had stayed in Somalia he might have had to join the army, so Mohammed decided to go to India. He was soon able to get a visa which allowed him to travel to India as a student.

A seventeenth-century painting of Malik Ambar (1550–1626).

It was the first time Mohammed had left his country and been on a plane. After a six-hour flight he arrived in Bombay, one of India's largest cities. After two days he went to Boona, a town in the state of Maharashtra near Bombay. There Mohammed rented a room in a house with other Somali students.

There are many Somalis in India, especially in the area around Bombay. This is the area in which people from Somalia and Ethiopia have settled for many hundreds of years. Most Somalis there today are students, but some Somali seamen have also settled in India and brought their families with them. Others are refugees from the civil war.

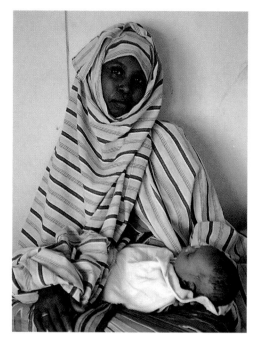

Many Somalis have fled their country because of war.

Somalis also migrate to the Middle East. This Somali is in Dubai, UAE.

Mohammed went to a college in Boona where he learnt English. He also had to try to learn Marathi, the local Indian language. Although he stayed in India for nearly two years, he always found this language very hard.

The Somali students in India all try to keep in touch with their country. They often live together or in the same area, and regularly meet up. Somalis always gather to celebrate Independence Day on June 26 each year.

It took Mohammed some time to get used to life in India, but he made a lot of Indian friends and he hopes to visit India again in the future.

As we have seen, Africans and people whose families originally came from Africa now live in many different parts of the world. Africans have become migrants for different reasons. In the past some were forced to migrate because they were taken away as slaves.

African culture has influenced the cultures of many countries. These girls are dancing at a festival in Cuba.

In modern times some Africans have migrated to find work or to get an education, and then remained abroad. Others have had to leave their own countries because of war or famine. Very often African migrations first take place within Africa. Refugees try to go to nearby countries within the continent. People seeking work also move to other African countries. Many more stay in their own countries, but move from one area to another.

When Africans migrate they naturally take their culture with them. Even centuries of slavery in the Americas did not completely destroy African cultures. The slaves and their descendants developed new languages, music and so on, wherever they were.

Modern African migrants also take their culture as well as their skills with them. Even if they can never return to Africa, through their culture they will always keep something from their homelands with them.

Glossary

African-American The name used to describe the black people of the USA. Many of these people's ancestors were once brought from Africa as slaves.

Apon A Nigerian food made from a kind of nut mixed with palm oil.

Bantu The name given to a family of African languages widely spoken in the southern half of the continent. In many of these languages the word means 'people'.

Creole A word often used to describe the languages of the Caribbean, which may be a mixture of African and European languages. The word 'patois' is also sometimes used.

Culture A people or country's way of life, including language, dress, food and customs.

Diaspora Originally a word used to describe the dispersal of Jewish people throughout the world, it is now also used to describe the world-wide dispersal of Africans.

Discrimination Treating a certain group of people unfairly because of negative feelings about their skin colour, language, religion or political beliefs.

Eba Nigerian food made by mixing ground cassava and water.

Ewedu A vegetable similar to spinach.

Horn of Africa The north-eastern part of Africa, which sticks out like a horn on the map. It includes countries such as Eritrea, Ethiopia and Somalia.

Immigrant A person who leaves his or her own country and goes to live in another one.

Industrial Revolution The growth of modern factories and transport which first took place in Britain from around 1750.

Injera Flat bread eaten by Ethiopians and Eritreans.

Ku-Klux-Klan A secret organization in the USA, formed by whites in the southern states in the nineteenth century. It uses violence against blacks and other minority groups.

Maroons The name given to runaway slaves in Jamaica and some other countries.

Obeah An African word still used in Jamaica meaning the use of spells and magic.

Osofu A Jamaican Maroon word for a village council.

Patois (see Creole)

Rastafarian The name comes from Ras Tafari, the last Ethiopian emperor, before he became known as Haile Selassie. Selassie is still thought of by many Rastafarians as a god.

Refugee Someone who has fled from his or her country and been accepted by the government of a new country because the person has a 'well-founded fear of being persecuted for reasons of race, religion, nationality etc' (UN Convention on Refugees, 1951).

Underground Railroad The organization that helped slaves in the USA to escape north to freedom. It included guides called conductors and safe houses called stations, where slaves could hide on their journey.

Zegni An Ethiopian sauce of pepper and spices eaten with *injera*.

Find out more

Books to read

These are some of the very few books which introduce Africa's history to children. Recommended reading age appears after each entry.

Chapter 1
Discovering Africa's Past by Basil Davidson (Longman, 1978)
An excellently-written and illustrated introduction to the whole history of the continent. Also contains some information on Africans in the Americas. 14-16; teachers

Roots of Racism and *Patterns of Racism* (Institute of Race Relations, 1982) Two books with useful information on the slave trade, colonialism and racism. Secondary

Chapters 2-3
Afro-American Music by Clive D. Griffin (Dryad, 1987) Descibes the African influences in the music and instruments of the Americas. 14-17

Four textbooks written for KS3 of the National Curriculum:
Britain and the Black Peoples of the Americas 1550-1930 by Joan Tucker (Jet, 1992)
Black Peoples in the Americas by Marika Sherwood and Bob Rees (Heinemann, 1992)
Black Peoples of the Americas 1500-1900s by Donald Hinds (Collins, 1993)
Black Peoples of the Americas by Nigel Smith (OUP, 1992)

Caribbean Food and Drink by Aviva Paraiso (Wayland, 1988) Includes information on African-influenced food in the Caribbean and recipes.

Caribbean Stories retold by Robert Hull (Wayland, 1994)

Equiano's Travels edited by Paul Edwards (Heinemann, 1967) A shortened and illustrated version of Equiano's autobiography. Secondary

Nanny of the Maroons and Tacky - Freedom Fighter and Folk Hero (Handprint, 1990) Two short story books for children about African leaders in Jamaica. Available from Handprint, 9 Key Hill Drive, Hockley, Birmingham B18 5NY, England

The People Who Came (3 books) edited by E.K. Brathwaite (Longman Caribbean, 1989) General history. Secondary

West Indian Folk Tales retold by Phillip Sherlock (OUP, 1966) Contains a number of Anansi stories from the West Indies.

These books from the USA may also be available in Britain:

Black Americans of Achievement series (Chelsea House, New York) contains a number of well-illustrated biographies for teenagers and young adults. These include Paul Cuffe, Benjamin Banneker, George Washington Carver, Marcus Garvey, Sojourner Truth, Harriet Tubman, Nat Turner and Denmark Vesey.

Chapters 4-6
The Somali Sailors by Similola Coker (booklet available from Ethnic Communities Oral History Project, 2 Royal Parade, Dawes Rd, London SW6 7RE) About the Somali community in Britain.

Further information for teachers

The African Heritage of American English by J.E. Holloway and W.K. Vans (Indiana University Press, 1993)

African Presence in Early America edited by I. Van Sertima (Transaction, 1992)

The Black Book by M. A. Harris et al. (Random House, New York, 1974) A largely pictorial account of African-American history.

Black Peoples in the Americas - A Handbook for Teachers by M. Sherwood (Savannah Press, 1992) Maps, photos, primary sources and teachers' notes.

Eyewitness: The Negro in American History by W.L. Katz (Pitman, 1968) Documentary sources of African-American history.

Folk Culture of the Slaves in Jamaica by E.K. Braithwaite (New Beacon, 1981)

Maroon Societies - Rebel Slave Communities in the Americas edited by R. Price (Anchor, 1973); republished 1993

Roots by Alex Haley (Hutchinson, 1977)

Soul Food by S. Ferguson (Weidenfeld and Nicolson, 1986) Recipes and information on the food of the southern USA.

The Travels of William Wells Brown: Narrative of William W. Brown Fugitive Slave; The American Fugitive in Europe; Sketches of People and Places Abroad ed. P. Jefferson (Edinburgh University Press, 1991)

You can listen to *Go Down Moses* and other spirituals on Paul Robeson's *Songs of Free Men* (CBS LP record MP 39512, 1968)

Index

Entries in **bold** indicate subjects shown in pictures as well as in the text.

NOTES ON SOURCES
1 *African Presence in Early America* ed. I Van Sertima (Transaction, 1992)
2 *Forced Migration: The Impact of the Export Slave Trade on African Societies* ed. by J E Inikori (Hutchison, London, 1982)
3 From *The Travels of William Wells Brown* ed. P Jefferson (Edinburgh University Press, 1991)
4 From *Folk Culture of the Slaves in Jamaica* by E.K. Braithwaite (New Beacon, 1981)

PICTURE ACKNOWLEDGEMENTS
A Abdulhay 38 (below); Archiv für Kunst und Geschichte 9, 12, 27; Associated Press 31; Bettmann Archive 16, 17; Bridgeman 14; Camera Press 23 (below); Robert Estall (C Beckwith) 2-3; Eye Ubiquitous (M Jeliffe) 19, 20 (above), 29 (above), 30, (T Page) 45; Fotomas Index 10; Frank Spooner Pictures (T Engstrom/ Gamma Liaison) 22; S and R Greenhill 33 (below); Robert Harding (Atkins) 6, 11, 18, 29 (below), 37 (above), 44 (above); Hull City Museums 28; Hutchison Library 36; Mansell 26; Museum of Fine Arts, Boston 43; Peter Newark 15, 16; C Osborne 34, 38 (above); Photri 20 (below), 21 (both), 24 (above); Peter Sanders 37 (below), 39; O Showunmi 32, 33 (above), 35; Tony Stone Worldwide 7; UNHCR (A Hollmann) 40 and 44; TRIP (M O'Brien) 41, (H Roger) 44 (below); UPI/Bettmann 24 (below); Wayland (Z Mukhida) *cover* and 23 (above).
Artwork: *cover* Simon Borrough; maps on pages 4-5, 6-7, 8, 13 and 25 by Peter Bull.